How we USE materials

Paper

Holly Wallace

Smart Apple Media

This book has been published in cooperation with Franklin Watts.

Series designed and created for Franklin Watts by Painted Fish Ltd.,
Art director: Jonathan Hair, Designer: Rita Storey, Editor: Fiona Corbridge

Picture credits
Corbis Sygma/Annebicque Bernard p. 9 (top), Corbis/Ariel Skelley p. 16, p. 27
(bottom); istockphoto.com p. 8, p. 9 (bottom), p. 13, p. 15, p. 17 (bottom), p. 18,
p. 19 (top), p. 21, p. 25, p. 26, p. 27 (top); Tudor Photography p. 3, p. 5, pp. 6–7,
pp. 10–11, p. 12, p. 14, p. 17 (top), p. 19 (bottom), p. 20, p. 22, p. 23, p. 24.

Cover images: Tudor Photography, Banbury

Published in the United States by Smart Apple Media
2140 Howard Drive West, North Mankato, Minnesota 56003

Library of Congress Cataloging-in-Publication Data

Wallace, Holly, 1961–
Paper / by Holly Wallace.
p. cm. — (How we use materials)
Includes index.
ISBN-13: 978-1-59920-004-0
1. Papermaking—Juvenile literature. I. Title.

TS1105.5.W36 2002
676—dc22   2006034719

9 8 7 6 5 4 3 2 1

Contents

Words in **bold** are in the glossary.

What is paper?

Paper is a **material**. It can be used to make many different things.

● Cards, envelopes, books, and newspapers are all made from paper.

● Paper objects, such as these bags and wrapping paper, can be **printed** with different colors and patterns.

● Tissues are made from soft, thin paper, which can soak up, or **absorb**, liquids well.

● Paper cups and plates can be used once and thrown away.

Paper keywords

Soft
Printed
Material
Absorb

Where does paper come from?

We make paper from tiny **fibers** that come from wood.

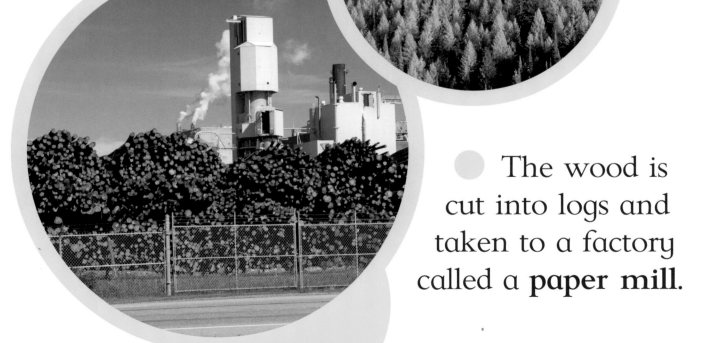

The wood is cut into logs and taken to a factory called a **paper mill**.

Here the wood is chopped into tiny pieces called chips. The chips are mixed with water and **chemicals**. Then machines mash them into a thick paste called **pulp**.

The pulp is spread out in a thin layer on a machine and dried to make paper. The finished paper is put on big rolls or cut into sheets.

Paper keywords

Fibers
Paper mill
Pulp

What is paper like?

Paper is used in many ways. Different kinds of paper are useful for different jobs.

Paper can be made into thin, smooth sheets that are used for writing. Paper can also be bent and folded to make envelopes for letters.

Colored paper is made by adding chemicals called **dyes** to the paper pulp.

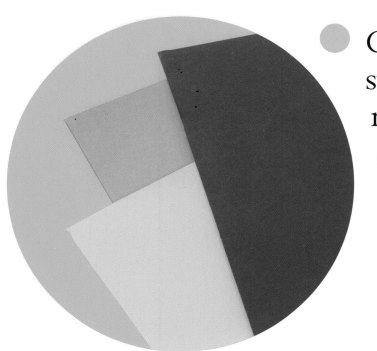

Cardstock is thick, stiff paper. It can be made in many different colors.

Cardboard is made from layers of cardstock and paper. Cardboard is stronger than ordinary paper and does not tear as easily. Cardboard is used to make boxes because it is thick and strong.

Paper keywords
Dyes
Cardboard
Cardstock

Paper for writing and painting

Paper is a good material for writing and painting on. Ink and paint stick to paper well.

Writing paper has a special smooth **coating**. The ink sticks to the coating and does not soak into the paper.

If you write on paper with a pencil, you can use an eraser to rub out any mistakes.

Some artists use paints called watercolors. They paint on special thick paper that absorbs the paint.

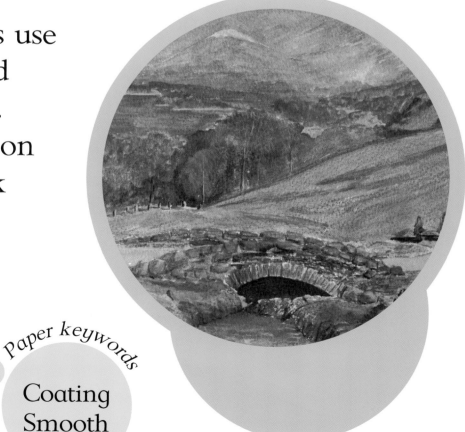

Paper keywords

Coating
Smooth

Paper for printing

Most paper is used for printing books, newspapers, and magazines.

● The pages inside a book are printed on book paper. This kind of paper is thin and white. The book's cover is made of cardboard. It **protects** the pages and holds them together.

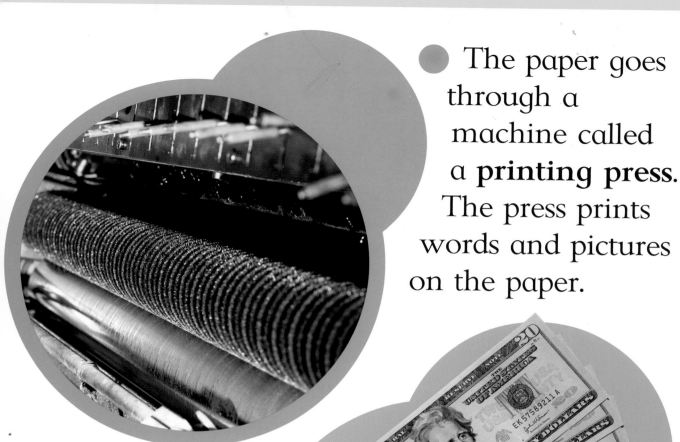

The paper goes through a machine called a **printing press**. The press prints words and pictures on the paper.

Paper money is printed on paper that has strong fibers in it. This makes the paper difficult to tear, so the money lasts longer.

Paper keywords
Printing
Printing press
Paper money

Wrapping paper

Some kinds of paper are used for wrapping presents or for sending packages by mail.

Paper is good for wrapping things because it is easy to cut and fold. Tape or glue can be used to stick pieces of paper together.

Wrapping paper comes in many different colors. Some paper has patterns and pictures printed on it.

Mr. J. Green
12 Park Terrace
Anytown, MN 12345

Miss S. Percy
23 Silver Street
Anytown, MN 12345

Brown paper has fibers from cotton plants added to it. This makes it stronger. Brown paper is good for wrapping packages that will be sent through the mail.

Paper keywords

Wrapping Colors

Paper packaging

Factories use paper and cardstock to hold and protect the things they make. This is called **packaging**.

- Strong cardboard boxes are used to hold heavy things, such as computers and televisions. The cardboard helps to keep the things inside from getting broken.

Some boxes are made from pulp that has been shaped in a **mold**. Egg cartons are a special shape to keep the eggs from moving around.

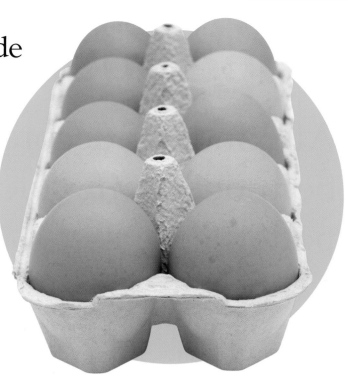

We buy milk and fruit juice in **cartons** made from thin cardboard. Cardboard is not **waterproof**. It must be coated with **wax** so that the liquid does not soak through it.

Paper keywords

Cartons
Waterproof
Packaging

Paper decorations

All kinds of decorations can be made from colored and patterned paper.

- We can make **paper chains** to decorate a room for a party. It is fun to use **paper streamers** like these.

- Party plates and cups are made from thin cardboard. They are **disposable**, and can be thrown away after use.

These model ducks are made from **papier mâché**. It is made from wet paper and glue. When it dries, it hardens.

Paper can be folded into all kinds of shapes, such as this animal. Folding paper into shapes is called **origami**.

Paper keywords

Disposable
Papier mâché
Origami

Paper in the home

Paper is good for decorating homes. It is also very useful in the kitchen.

- Walls can be covered with **wallpaper** instead of paint. Wallpaper is a thick and heavy paper that comes in rolls. It is printed with different patterns and colors. It is glued onto a wall.

Paper towels, paper napkins, tissues, and toilet paper are made from paper that is good at soaking up liquids.

Sandpaper is made by gluing sand onto tough paper, which gives it a rough surface. Sandpaper is used to make wood smooth and to rub away old paint.

Paper keywords

Wallpaper
Sandpaper

Paper at school

Look around your classroom. You use lots of paper objects at school.

- You write in notebooks made of paper. Teachers make lists and posters out of paper and cardboard and hang them on the wall.

To print out words or pictures from a computer, you need a printer filled with sheets of paper.

Is your classroom decorated with paintings and collages?
A collage is a picture made from glued paper shapes.

Paper keywords
Printer
Paintings
Collages

Recycling paper

Millions of tons of paper are thrown away every day. But most of this could be **recycled**.

Old paper is collected for recycling. It is mashed up to make pulp. This is mixed with new pulp and made into new paper.

Most recycled paper is used to make cardboard and newspapers. Some is used to make tissues, paper towels, and toilet paper.

Paper can also be reused. One way to reuse old newspaper is to tear it into strips and use it to make cozy bedding for a pet.

Paper keywords
Recycled
Mashed
Tear

Glossary

Absorb Soak up liquids.

Brown paper Thick, strong paper made with cotton fibers. It is used for wrapping packages.

Cardboard A type of thin board made from layers of cardstock and paper.

Cartons Boxes made from light cardboard that are used for holding milk, fruit juice, and other types of food and drink.

Chemicals Special substances used to do many jobs, such as making wood softer to make paper.

Coating An outer layer.

Disposable Designed to be thrown away after use.

Dyes Substances used to color paper.

Fibers Very thin threads. The fibers in paper come from trees and plants.

Material Something out of which other objects can be made.

Mold A shape that pulp is poured into to make the same shape.

Origami A special way of folding paper to make it into objects and decorations. It started in Japan.

Packaging Boxes, cartons, and envelopes in which other objects are packed. Factories also use paper and cardboard packaging to protect the things they make when they are sold in stores.

Paper chains Decorations made from a chain of paper loops.

Paper mill A factory where paper is made.

Paper money Pieces of paper that are worth a certain amount of money.

Paper streamers Long, thin pieces of paper used as decorations.

Papier mâché A material made from wet paper and glue that hardens when it dries.

Printed Marked with words or pictures.

Printing press A machine that marks paper with words or pictures.

Protects Keeps something from getting dirty or spoiled.

Pulp A mixture of wood chips, water, and chemicals that has been mashed together.

Recycled Used materials that have been collected so that they can be specially treated and used again.

Wallpaper Large sheets of colored or patterned paper that can be pasted on to walls to decorate them.

Waterproof Does not let water pass through.

Wax A smooth, oily material that does not let liquid pass through it.

Index